COWGIRL UP
COLORING BOOK

by
Terry L. Duke

TO: _____

FROM: _____

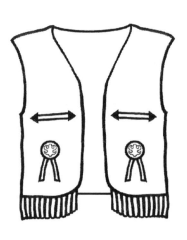

The whole Armor of God –

I must **dress** in it daily!

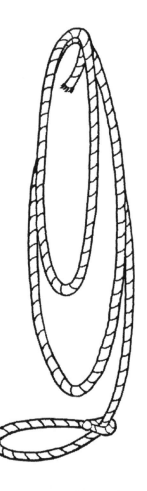

The **helmet** of Salvation

I have asked Jesus into my heart.

I put on the **helmet** of Salvation.

The helmet protects and guards my mind.

Scripture: John 3:16; Ephesians 6:17

The **breastplate** of Righteousness

I am in Right Standing with God,

because I am His child.

I wear a **breastplate** of Righteousness.

Scripture: Ephesians 6:14

Truth around my waist

I read and study God's Word

to put the Truth in my heart.

Truth makes me free.

I put Truth around my waist.

Scripture: Ephesians 6:14

The **shoes** of Peace

I wear **shoes** of Peace. Jesus is Peace.

I am quick to go share Jesus (Peace)

with others.

Scripture: Ephesians 6:15

The **shield** of Faith

I carry a **shield** of Faith.

The shield puts out ALL the fiery darts

of the devil.

Scripture: Ephesians 6:16

The **sword** of the Spirit

I have a **sword** of the Spirit,

which is the Word of God.

I use the sword to fight all my battles.

Scripture: Ephesians 6:17

I now wear the

whole Armor of God!

For God so loved the world, that he gave his only begotten Son, that whosoever believeth in him should not perish, but have everlasting life.

– John 3:16 **KJV**

For God so loved the world, that He gave His only begotten Son, that whoever believes in Him should not perish, but have eternal life.

– John 3:16 **NAS**

For God so greatly loved and dearly prized the world that He [even] gave up His only begotten ([a]unique) Son, so that whoever believes in (trusts in, clings to, relies on) Him shall not perish (come to destruction, be lost) but have eternal (everlasting) life.

– John 3:16 **Amplified**

Heavenly Father,

I come to You in the name of Jesus.
I believe Jesus came in the flesh. I believe
Jesus died on the cross for my sins, and
after three days, He rose again from the
dead. I now ask You into my heart.
I believe You told the truth. Thank You
for hearing me, and coming into my heart.
Thank You for forgiving me of my sins.
I now choose You to be the Lord of my life.
Thank You for being my Daddy and
making me Your child from this day forward.
In Jesus' name,

Amen

About the Author

Terry L. Duke is a wife, mother, grandmother and great-grandmother. She is a career registered nurse specializing in Diabetes Education. As a born-again Christian for many years, Terry's ultimate goal is to complete her earthly race by telling others about Jesus and His love for them. She is a graduate of Rhema Bible Training College.

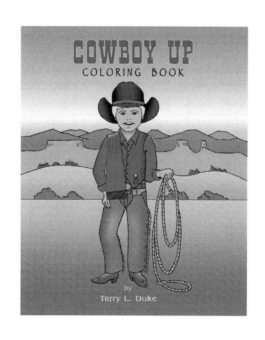

Also available from Terry L. Duke –
COWBOY UP
book and coloring book.
Go to **amazon.com**
for ordering information.

The whole Armor of God –
I must **dress** in it daily!

Made in the USA
Columbia, SC
20 August 2024

40348797R00015